Ann Story

Vermont's Heroine of Independence

Ann Story

Vermont's Heroine of Independence

MICHAEL T. HAHN

THE NEW ENGLAND PRESS, INC.
SHELBURNE, VERMONT

Manufactured in the United States of America
Second Printing, July 1998
Third Printing, July 2004

Cover illustration by Elayne Sears

For additional copies of this book or for a
catalog of our other titles, please write:

The New England Press
P.O. Box 575
Shelburne, VT 05482

or e-mail info@nepress.com

Visit our website at www.nepress.com

Hahn, Michael, 1953-
    Ann Story : Vermont's heroine of independence / Michael Hahn.
      p. cm.
    Includes bibliographical references.
    Summary: Biography of the Vermonter who was known as the "Mother of the Green Mountain Boys" and who was one of the few women whose contributions to the Patriot cause were documented.
    ISBN 1-881535-16-9
    1. Story, Ann, 1742-1817--Juvenile literature. 2. Heroines--Vermont--Biography--Juvenile literature. 3. Vermont--History--Revolution, 1775-1783--Juvenile literature. 4. United States--History--Revolution, 1775-1783--Women--Juvenile literature.
[1. Story, Ann, 1742-1817. 2. Heroines. 3. Vermont--History--Revolution, 1775-1783. 4. Women--Biography.] I. Title.
E263.V5H34 1996
974.3'03'092--dc20
[B]   96-8255
                                            CIP
                                            AC

CONTENTS

INTRODUCTION

This is a biography of Ann Story, a remarkable woman who became famous for her bravery and patriotism. Ann was many things: a devoted mother, an expert with an ax, and an eager supporter of self-government. She was strong, resourceful, and trustworthy.

Ann Story and her husband Amos moved from Connecticut to a wild, unsettled area known as the New Hampshire Grants. When Amos Story died, leaving Ann with five children to raise, she refused to retreat from the hostile wilderness. She dug a secret hideaway where her family could sleep safely and remained on the frontier during the Revolutionary War.

The New Hampshire Grants later became the state of Vermont. When Ann first settled in the area, however, people disagreed about who owned the land. The settlers had bought their land from New Hampshire, but New York also claimed the area. Many of the people who lived in the Grants wanted to create a separate state instead of becoming a part of either New York or New Hampshire. The settlers in the Grants banded together and formed a group called the Green Mountain Boys to protect their land. The Green Mountain Boys defended the Grants homesteads against New York investors, who claimed the land for themselves.

By the time the American colonists declared independence from Great Britain, the Green Mountain Boys were an experienced group of fighters. Ann Story supported the Green Mountain Boys in their struggle against Britain. She once passed along information about a group of spies that led to their capture before they could deliver important intelligence to the British.

Many brave women helped settle the American frontier, but Ann Story stands out because of her contributions to the creation of Vermont and the birth of the United States of America. She was an inspirational woman who faced hard times with courage and honesty.

ANN'S YOUTH

Recorded details of Ann Story's early life are rare. Historians disagree on her birth date; some believe that she was born in 1735, while others claim it was 1741. This book will use the 1741 date to figure Ann's age, because that is the date written on her tombstone.

Ann was born in Preston, Connecticut, and named Hannah Reynolds. Her parents were Jonathan Reynolds and Hannah Tracy Reynolds. Jonathan and Hannah's children were named Jonathan, Samuel (who died as a baby), another Samuel, Christopher, Hannah, Ebenezer, and Jerusha. Hannah and Jerusha were the only girls. Because she had the same name as her mother, young Hannah was called Ann.

Ann was raised in a stern community. The Connecticut colonists were religious and strict. A person could be fined for saying "damn" or "go to the Devil." Laughing in church would get a person hauled off to court. All citizens had to pay a tax to provide for the minister, and anyone who did not pay the tax would be thrown in jail. If the prisoner still did not pay, a cow or some other property would be seized to cover the cost.

Preston was located near the larger town of Norwich, and together they formed a close-knit community. Strangers were forbidden to stay in town without permission, which was rarely granted. For a period of eighteen years, from 1751 to 1769, it was illegal for anyone to sell land in Norwich to a stranger.

During Ann's childhood, the New England colonies were changing, as attitudes eased from the harsh Puritan values. The Europeans who first came to New England had needed all their energy to build shelters and raise enough food to last through the long winters. Work and prayer had been their only activities. Many years later, after they had created villages, farms, and fields, people had more time to relax.

During Ann's youth, dancing became popular with respectable young folks. Singers and sometimes a fiddler played jigs, reels, minuets, and contra-dances. Weddings could feature huge dance parties that lasted for two days or longer, with more than two hundred dances performed.

On election days and other holidays, men and boys competed in sporting contests. Foot races, horse races, wrestling, jumping contests, and shooting competitions were all popular. Thanksgiving was a special holiday, with many festivities in addition to the sermon. One of Ann's favorite Thanksgiving treats was the barrel bonfire, in which a pyramid of tar-coated barrels was built around a tall pole. When it was set on fire, the spectacular blaze lit the entire town.

When the crops were harvested and snow covered the ground, many people enjoyed sleighing parties. Horses pulled sleighs across snow-covered roads, while the passengers shouted at each other and sometimes threw snowballs.

During warmer weather, rich ladies wore fancy gowns with long trains, which they carried over their right arm when walking. Silk stockings and high-heeled satin slippers were in style. Ladies often carried a large fan for shade and a breeze. Ruffles, silk scarves, and other elegant decorations graced the well-dressed ladies of colonial Connecticut.

Rich men also wore fancy clothes: silk suits with gold and silver embroidery, silver knee buckles, and bows on their shoes. Ministers and officials wore curled wigs, white with powder. Other men had their hair curled and powdered for special occasions.

Ann's family could not afford fancy clothes. As a poor man, her father was "bound out," or required to farm on another man's land. Ann had to settle for secondhand clothes, and she learned to work at an early age, helping with household chores.

Having five brothers and one sister, living in a close-knit community whose strict attitudes were easing, and being a member of a hard-working poor family all influenced Ann's personality. She became a tomboy, joining her brothers in boyish pursuits. She developed strong feelings of commitment to her family and community. Accepting hard work as a part of life, she never expected to get anything that she did not earn. These influences helped build the character of an amazing woman.

STARTING A FAMILY

Amos Story was born in Ipswich, Massachusetts, on September 12, 1731, which made him four to ten years older than Hannah Reynolds, depending on her uncertain birth date. History does not tell us how they met, but they were married in Norwich, Connecticut, on September 17, 1755. Ann was either fourteen or twenty years old when she married Amos. It was not unusual to get married at fourteen in those days, considering the generally shorter life spans of that time.

Amos and Ann's first son was born in 1761, and they named him Solomon. Another son was born two years later, named Ephraim. He was followed by a third son, Samuel, and two daughters, Susanna and Hannah. All five children were born in Connecticut. Although Amos and Ann were poor, they did everything they could to give their children a bright future. Amos was working as a "bound out" farmer, and the only way that he and Ann could improve the situation was for their family to become landowners.

During the pioneer years in America, a family's fortunes depended on farming enough land to raise plenty of crops and livestock. When an area was first settled, a couple could easily claim enough land for their family. A generation later, when their children married, the amount of land might still be adequate, but by the third generation the family would not have enough land for a comfortable life. When the area became thickly settled, the price of land rose beyond the reach of poor families. Instead of accepting poverty, a bold family could move to the frontier. By homesteading in a wilderness area, poor people could work their way into the middle class.

The chance of getting a better life through hard labor developed a strong work ethic in New England, where individual effort could lead to good fortune. Ann and Amos Story wanted a better life for their family, so they looked northward, toward the land of opportunity on the frontier.

THE NEW HAMPSHIRE
LAND GRANTS

B y the time Amos and Ann Story considered moving north of Connecticut, the area had been fought over for a long time. The Abenaki Indians had struggled against the English colonists of New England for almost a hundred years, defending their homeland. As allies of the French, the Abenaki fought the British during the French and Indian Wars. But the British eventually won, clearing the way for settlers from the English colonies in Massachusetts, Connecticut, and New York to pioneer northward.

Benning Wentworth, New Hampshire's first governor, granted land charters to homesteaders for many locations between Lake Champlain and the Connecticut River. Between 1749 and 1764, he granted about three million acres in 138 towns. Homesteaders moved into the area, clearing land and building settlements, and by the 1760s the region was known as the New Hampshire Grants.

The New Hampshire Grants also attracted the attention of the wealthy landowners in the colony of New York. New York's Governor Cadwallader Colden disputed New Hampshire's claim to the area, insisting that it was actually part of New York. Colden demanded that Governor Wentworth withdraw New Hampshire's claim.

The boundaries of the American colonies were not clearly defined at that time. The colonies had been granted by King George III of England, who had never been within two thousand miles of them. King George could not have known much about American geography, because the few maps of America that existed back then were not very accurate. The king had authorized the governor of each colony to grant land within his jurisdiction, and Governor Wentworth considered the New Hampshire Grants to be within his jurisdiction.

Since New Hampshire had once been a part of Massachusetts, Governor Wentworth believed that the western boundary of New Hampshire should be located in line with the western boundary of Massachusetts, which lay twenty miles east of the Hudson River. Governor Colden disagreed—he claimed that New York's jurisdiction extended east all the way to the Connecticut River.

In 1764, the year Ann and Amos Story were starting their family in Connecticut, Governor Wentworth and Governor Colden agreed to let King George decide who held legal title to the disputed area between Lake Champlain and the Connecticut River. The king ruled in favor of New York, declaring that the area known as the New Hampshire Grants was actually part of New York.

Governor Colden interpreted the King's decision to mean that all the grants that Governor Wentworth had issued in the past were worthless. He issued New York grants for many lots in the Bennington area that had already been purchased under New Hampshire grants.

By law, the king's decision should have been final. But the settlers in the New Hampshire Grants refused to give up their homes. About two hundred families already lived in the area. They had paid for their land in good faith and had worked hard, clearing land for fields and building log cabins. They were furious at the king's decision and were not willing to throw away their investment of money and hard work. When New York surveyors trespassed on Grants homesteads in 1765, angry Grants people petitioned the King of England to reverse his decision.

King George might have kept the dispute from boiling over if he had declared a settlement for the families who were homesteading in the Grants. But instead he stalled, claiming that the problem needed further study. In 1767 he ordered New York to stop issuing grants on land that was already claimed until the results of the further investigations came back.

The Grants settlers faced an unpleasant choice—they could either leave their homes or pay again for land they had already bought. To rebuy their own land, however, the price was steep. Governor Wentworth had charged twenty pounds per grant, but Governor Colden charged 200 to 250 pounds per grant, an impossible price for most families. Many settlers decided to defy the king and hold on to their homes by whatever means necessary.

New settlers took advantage of the uncertainty by buying land at low prices from real estate investors who were selling under old New Hampshire grants. Between 1767 and 1769, the area's population tripled. The New

York government was angered by the New Hampshire grant sales, and it issued new grants on land claimed by New Hampshire, ignoring the king's orders.

By the time Ann and Amos Story planned their move north in the early 1770s, the land dispute had not been settled. They were taking a risk when they bought land from a New Hampshire grant—but that was the least of their worries as they took up life in a dangerous wilderness.

TRAGEDY STRIKES

When a family moved from southern New England to settle in the Grants, they usually were separated during the first trip. The mother remained behind in the old home with the young children while the father traveled into the wilderness to build a cabin, clear land, and plant crops. The frontier was rough and dangerous, and most families did not want to risk moving the children until they had built a cabin to shelter them.

The settlers called creating a homestead "going to make their pitch." For safety reasons, a man would usually make his pitch with a helper or as part of a small group. When Amos Story was ready to go make his pitch in the Grants, his oldest son, Solomon, was thirteen years old. Ann and Amos agreed that Solomon was old enough to go into the wilderness to help prepare their new home. While Amos and Solomon went to make their pitch, the rest of the family moved to the Grants town of Rutland, where Ann and the younger children found a place to live.

Amos and Ann carefully chose equipment for the trip, packing an ax, auger, and whetstone for clearing the land and building the cabin. They packed wheat, corn, bean, and pumpkin seeds to plant crops. Other essential items included clothing, blankets, a kettle, and a "spider" (a frying pan with legs designed to stand over an open fire). Ann packed a small amount of food, but Amos and Solomon would rely mostly on hunting and fishing to feed themselves.

Ann and Amos bade each other farewell, and Ann watched her husband and oldest son leave for the wilderness.

Amos and Solomon had little trouble finding food. Moose, squirrels, turkeys, snowshoe hares, grouse, and deer were all abundant in the Grants, and the streams were full of colorful brook trout. After a pleasant journey, the travelers reached the town of Salisbury in September 1774.

Salisbury was one of the earliest towns in Addison County, having been chartered on November 3, 1761. But when Amos and Solomon arrived, it was a town in name only. So wild was the area that the proprietors' offer of one hundred acres per settler had not attracted a single homesteader in twelve years. Amos Story was only the second settler to make his pitch in Salisbury. The first settler in town, Joshua Graves, was living there with his son Jesse when Amos and Solomon came to the Otter Valley wilderness.

Amos found his hundred acres on the east shore of Otter Creek, on the southern border of the Graves property. Aside from the Graveses, Amos and Solomon were alone, with no one to rely on but themselves. Such solitude made Grants pioneers into independent and resourceful people.

As the leaves changed from green to the bright colors of fall, Amos and Solomon toppled large maples and oaks to clear the land. They chopped the tops and branches of the trees into firewood and saved the trunks for logs to build their cabin. They had no time to allow the logs to dry, which would have controlled warping, but instead had to work with green wood. Racing against the onset of winter, they started to build their new home.

Amos and Solomon worked through the winter, constructing a modest but sturdy cabin. By the spring of 1775, they had finished it—a snug shelter against the fickle Grants weather. Although the cabin was ready for Ann and the children, Amos and Solomon still had more work to do before they could fetch the rest of the family.

They had been living mostly on fish, which were abundant in Otter Creek, plus meat whenever they spared a little time to hunt. With no bread and little salt, however, their all-flesh diet was boring, and they needed to plant crops before departing for Rutland, so they started clearing land to plant wheat.

Their work went well for a while, as they felled the mighty hardwoods to let daylight into the forest. Father and son worked smoothly as a team, bonded by their common labor. Then one day disaster hit.

Amos was cutting down a large maple tree. He swung the ax powerfully, notching the trunk facing the area where he wanted the tree to fall. Then he started chopping through the opposite side of the trunk, slightly above the notch. As he whittled away at the trunk, the great tree slowly leaned toward the notch, groaning as it fought against gravity. Popping and cracking, the tree started to fall.

Amos moved away, retreating from danger as he had so many times before. But a limb high on the falling tree hit another tree, causing the falling tree to twist. A lower limb swung around and hit Amos, knocking him to the ground. Before he could get up, the maple tree smashed down on top of him.

Aghast, Solomon stared in shock at the big tree pinning his father to the earth. When he screamed at Amos, he received no reply. Driven by panic, the boy picked up the ax and hacked away at the tree. The maple's trunk was two feet thick, and it took a long time for him to chop through the hardwood. His father never moved.

When Solomon had finally cut through the tree, he tried to roll the trunk off Amos, but he could not budge it. Fighting back tears, the boy picked up the ax again and chopped through the trunk on the other side of his father. Then, exhausted, he rolled the short section of log off his father.

Staring at his father's crushed body, Solomon realized he was alone in the wilderness. No one was living at the Graves farm at the moment, since Joshua and Jesse had returned to their home in Arlington for the winter. The nearest neighbors lived far away in Middlebury. Solomon ran for miles through the woods to the home of Benjamin Smalley and choked out the tragic news.

Benjamin Smalley and his two sons Imri and Alfred went with Solomon back to the Story homestead. They carried Amos's body to the burial plot where Benjamin's two daughters were buried—Benjamin's daughter Anna had become lost in the forest and died from starvation at the age of twenty, and her sister Zerah had died from a fever at the age of eighteen. Solomon and the Smalleys laid Amos to rest beside the Smalley girls, just north of the Middlebury River. After thanking the Smalleys for their help, Solomon walked to Rutland alone to deliver the terrible news to his mother.

When her teenage son returned from the wilderness alone, Ann Story learned that she was a widow with an uncertain future. Most women in her situation would have retreated to the comfort of family and friends in Connecticut, but Ann was a bold and stubborn woman. She decided to continue her plans to move her family into the New Hampshire Grants.

PERSEVERANCE

According to most accounts, Ann Story was thirty-three years old when she became a widow, the mother of five children. Solomon, her oldest, was fourteen years old, and her youngest, Hannah, was only three. Moving her family into the wilderness, where they would be entirely on their own, was an awesome task, yet Ann did not hesitate to take it on.

A tall, healthy, athletic woman, Ann's physical strength was only one of the special qualities that helped her to consider such a bold plan. Her mental strengths were equally impressive: she was wise, trustworthy, and honest. And of course she was brave, or she would never have continued to Salisbury.

To raise money, Ann sold most of her household belongings, keeping only the basics for herself and her children, including a family Bible. With the money she purchased a packhorse to carry goods to their new home.

In the spring of 1775, Ann loaded her packhorse with supplies, including salt, flour, bacon, gunpowder, lead bullets, blankets, seed, and the few pieces of extra clothing that her family still owned. She and Solomon both carried long rifles. Familiar with guns, she was considered a fair shot and was also handy with an ax, knew how to roll logs with a lever, and could do other tasks usually associated with men.

When Ann and her children began their journey north, they left Rutland, crossed the edge of the frontier in Pittsford, and traveled deep into the wilderness to Salisbury. They spent one night at Benjamin Smalley's cabin, where Ann stopped to mourn at her husband's grave. After thanking Smalley for his help, the Story family continued traveling, with no one to depend on but themselves.

Solomon led his mother to their cabin near the bank of Otter Creek. When Ann looked at the cabin that her late husband had built with honest sweat, she knew that she had made the right decision by coming there. The building was modest, and the ragged clearing was overgrown with brambles, but the rough homestead gave her children a chance for a better life. She and her husband had planned to raise their children as free citizens of the New Hampshire Grants, and even now she was determined to see their dream fulfilled.

The family dusted out the cabin and moved in, then immediately began chopping the brambles and weeds from their precious crops. Cutworms and other pests were a serious problem, and the family had to constantly defend their fields against them. Even the youngest children helped with the chores. Ann maintained a pleasant, positive outlook, but kept her rifle close at hand. She and Solomon fed the family venison, bear meat, and fish until the crops matured. They gathered a modest harvest in the fall.

During the previous decade many settlers had migrated to the Otter Creek Valley. By 1775 at least a family or two had homesteaded in every town along the creek. But around the time that the Storys arrived, the settlers stopped moving in and many who had come left their homes for safer areas to the south. There were no other women and children in the entire region during the winter of 1775–1776 because they had moved out of the area for protection.

The cabin of their only neighbor, Joshua Graves, was vacant that winter, so the Storys were in fact the only inhabitants of Salisbury. The winter was long and cold, with very deep snow. Wolves howled outside the cabin some nights, and the threat of a hungry catamount was always there, as well as hostile Indians on the prowl. The family's small supply of food barely lasted the winter, but they survived.

During the winter months, huddled near the fireplace for warmth, Ann taught her children to read from the Bible. She explained to them the importance of setting themselves up as landowners, so they could become free citizens.

When the tough grip of winter finally began to loosen, Ann and the children tapped some of their maple trees and boiled the sap into maple syrup. As they flavored their Indian corn mush with the sweet syrup, Ann knew that spring was just around the corner, and she gave a prayer of thanks.

Still, the Champlain Valley and Otter Creek were dangerous places during the spring of 1776, due to some important events at Lexington, Concord, and Ticonderoga. Ann Story and her children were living in the path of violence.

STATE OF TURMOIL

In 1775 the English colonies in America were defying the policies of the English government, especially
the practice of taxation without representation. The
American colonists had nobody at the English Parliament
in London to speak on their behalf, and every time they
protested against taxes, London reacted harshly, causing more protests. Many New England citizens were
ready to cut their ties with King George III altogether.
The idea of freedom from foreign rule was particularly
pleasing to many settlers in the New Hampshire Grants,
whose homes were threatened by the king's decision to
favor New York's claim to the land.

That spring, in the Grants town of Westminster, several local settlers were worried that they might lose their
homes. A poor harvest the previous fall had made it dif-
ficult for them to pay their debts, so they were in danger
of losing everything they owned. On March 13, 1775,

the threatened farmers took over the Westminster court-house to prevent any civil hearings against them.

The local sheriff, William Paterson, worked for the New York authorities. He led a posse of twenty-five armed men to the courthouse and demanded that the farmers leave. They refused. Paterson led his men away, but he brought his posse back at midnight and ordered them to shoot at the men inside the courthouse, who were armed only with clubs. When the shooting was over, twelve set-tlers were wounded, two of them fatally. More farmers were thrown into jail.

News of the massacre spread swiftly throughout the surrounding countryside, and hundreds of Green Moun-tain Boys assembled in Westminster the following night. The Green Mountain Boys were Grants men who pa-trolled the area to defend Grants citizens against New York surveyors and posses. In Westminster they freed the farmers and captured the sheriff and several mem-bers of his posse, sending them to New York to stand trial for murder. New York officials later released Paterson and his men, which infuriated the Westminster settlers.

Ann Story, shocked by the Westminster massacre, be-lieved that Paterson and his posse should have been tried for murder. The fact that New York had released men who had killed defenseless Grants settlers made her de-termined to help the Green Mountain Boys in any way she could.

Tensions were running high throughout America. Ten thousand British soldiers were stationed in the colonies, and many Americans considered them an occupying army that forced British authority on them. The Ameri-cans were prepared for trouble; rebellious citizens from all walks of life who longed to be free of the king's rule donated time, money, and goods to produce a stockpile of supplies. Concord and Worcester, two towns close to Boston, were among the most important storage areas where they hid food, gunpowder, cannons, cannon balls, lead shot, and other supplies. In April 1775 patriot spies discovered that seven hundred British redcoats were headed to Concord to destroy the supplies there.

On April 19, a small force of patriots waited for the British in Lexington, a town between Boston and Concord. At dawn, about seventy-five militiamen braced themselves on the Lexington Green as seven hundred redcoats approached. Both the militia and the British troops were under strict orders not to fire the first shot. No one knows who disobeyed those orders, but someone did. After the first shot, the British troops fired two devastating volleys at the rebels. Within only a few minutes, eight Americans were dead and nine or ten others were wounded. One British soldier and a horse received slight wounds. The British continued their march toward Concord.

News of the British march traveled quickly through the surrounding countryside, and militias from nearby towns assembled to march toward Concord. Meanwhile the supplies in Concord were hidden or loaded onto carts to be hauled to safety. Although the militia force increased to about 150 men, they were still greatly outnumbered and retreated as the British entered Concord.

The British lingered in Concord, expecting to be joined by reinforcements from Boston. More and more patriots arrived from nearby towns, however, and eventually the patriots outnumbered the redcoats. Around noon the British retreated from Concord. Some of the militia cut across fields to circle ahead of the British, setting up ambushes on the road to Boston. Patriots hid beside the road, shot at the British from cover, then ran ahead to find another ambush site. A deadly crossfire came at the British soldiers from both sides of the road, and they fled. They met their reinforcements near Lexington, but they continued to retreat toward Boston anyway.

The British suffered more than 270 casualties at Lexington and Concord (including killed, wounded, and missing), while the patriots suffered fewer than one hundred. These battles stirred the American colonies into full-scale revolution.

Ann Story was thrilled by the patriot success in these battles. A strong believer in self-government and independence, she knew that the colonists' defiance had now bloomed into a commitment to fight for their liberty. She and Amos had bought their land through a New Hampshire Grant, which the King of England had declared worthless. Ann refused to give up her land and her dream without a fight, so she supported the patriots' cause. She knew that the Green Mountain Boys were the strongest group of rebels in her area, and she was willing to risk almost anything to help them.

When Ethan Allen, the colorful leader of the Green Mountain Boys, heard about the battles at Lexington and Concord, he saw a way to help the patriot cause. He knew that Fort Ticonderoga controlled the important Champlain Valley, and he led his men in an attempt to capture the fort and strike a blow for American independence.

Ethan Allen and the Green Mountain Boys achieved a major accomplishment by capturing Fort Ticonderoga without the loss of a single life on either side. The many artillery pieces they captured, moreover, played an important role in the war for independence—the following January, George Washington used Fort Ticonderoga artillery to bombard the British out of Boston. Their victory showed the world that the American rebels had a chance against the powerful British Empire.

While the Green Mountain Boys and other American patriots were defying Great Britain, Ann Story was building a home for her family on Otter Creek. She was eager to do her part for independence and liberty. Fate soon gave her that chance.

STANDING HER GROUND

Ann Story's wilderness home now became even
more dangerous. In January 1776 a man in Philadelphia named Thomas Paine published a pamphlet
called *Common Sense* that further fanned the fires of
rebellion. The pamphlet, easy to read and understand,
criticized King George III and the very idea of monar-
chy, then called for American independence and self-
government. About 150,000 copies of *Common Sense*
were sold, and the profits went to the Continental Congress to help pay for the revolution.

By February, General George Washington had assembled more than seventeen thousand patriots under
his command, and this Continental Army drove the British troops from Boston in March. But then the war worsened for the rebels as American troops trying to drive
the British out of Canada failed to conquer Quebec. The
arrival of British reinforcements, plus a shortage of supplies, doomed the invasion of Canada. The Americans

retreated to Fort Ticonderoga, where smallpox and other diseases, plus a lack of food, ammunition, and other supplies, sent morale sinking so low that many men deserted.

The weakening American military position left the Grants region unprotected. The British military leaders in Canada gave arms and supplies to their fierce Indian allies and encouraged the Indians to raid the settlements of northern New England. The Grants settlers had two reactions to these terrifying developments: any trace of Loyalist sympathy (loyalty to the king) disappeared, and almost all the settlers retreated to the larger towns to the south. Few settlers dared to remain on their lonely homesteads while bands of Indians were raiding the area.

Ann knew about the danger and did not want to put her children at risk, but she was also unwilling to leave her home. She had invested everything she owned in the homestead, and Amos had died while creating it. Determined to keep her home, she decided to face the danger head-on.

The Story cabin was located on Otter Creek, an important canoe route between Lake Champlain and the Green Mountains. Indians of various tribes paddled on Otter Creek sometimes, as well as Whigs (who wanted independence from England) and Tories (who were loyal to the king). Before roads were built, lakes and streams were the best "highways" in the Grants.

The Story home was also located on the front lines of the war. As the Green Mountain Boys defended the New England citizens against the British Army in Canada, Ann Story was in a position to aid their fight for liberty.

Legend has it that when Ann Story volunteered to actively help the Green Mountain Boys, she said: "I cannot live to see my children murdered before my eyes—

give me a place among you and see if I am the first to desert my post." Maybe she really said this, or maybe someone invented it to make her tale more interesting, but it is the most famous quote attributed to her. Whether she said it or not, she definitely volunteered her services to the Green Mountain Boys.

The fact that all her neighbors had fled the area made Ann's position even more valuable to the cause. Her home became an outpost for the Green Mountain Boys, a place where patriots could find rest and shelter. The cabin also served as a message drop, where a traveling patriot could leave intelligence information to be passed along. Finally, the Green Mountain Boys used it as a supply depot, storing ammunition and other equipment there.

One day in the spring of 1776, one of Ann's sons saw smoke rising from the cabin of Joshua Graves. Their neighbor and his son had left the cabin the previous September, seeking safety to the south. When Ann looked at the smoke a half-mile away, she realized that it was not smoke from a chimney—the Graves cabin was burning!

A raiding party of Indians had traveled from Canada, with the blessings of the British military officers, to loot and burn the deserted houses on the Grants frontier. Ann had been dreading their arrival. Reacting quickly, she urged her children to gather their possessions. Everything of value that they could carry was loaded into their canoe, including tools, utensils, clothing, and stores of maple sugar, corn, and bear fat.

The canoe, heavy with all the goods plus Ann and her five children, rode dangerously low in the water. She paddled carefully across Otter Creek to the Cornwall side. Snow melt and spring rains had left the stream high and muddy. The water had risen above the banks of Otter Creek, flooding the forest on the far shore. Ann steered the canoe into this flooded swamp, gliding into the middle of a thick brush patch.

Peeking out from her hiding place, Ann watched flames shoot high into the air above the Graves cabin. She prayed that the Indians would leave without discovering her home, but they found it with a whoop. Hushing her children, squeezing the younger ones tightly, she tried to comfort them as they all watched the Indians search and wreck their homestead. Ann wanted to scream when they set fire to the house, but she bit her lip. The cabin went up in smoke.

After the Indians left, Ann hid in the flooded trees for a long time before she dared come out. Finally she paddled back across Otter Creek and pulled ashore at her ruined homestead. Discouraged, she surveyed the smoking, charred ruins of her home. An ordinary person would have fled to safety, but Ann squared her shoulders, thanked God that none of the children had been harmed, and set out to rebuild. She knew that the Indians had found little of value in her home and the Graves cabin, and she hoped that this would discourage them from raiding them again.

Ann and the children immediately started to cut down trees for a new cabin. Since they had neither a team of oxen nor a lot of manpower, they selected smaller trees that they could move by hand. They rebuilt on the same spot where the first cabin had stood. According to a story that generations of the Story family have handed down, Ann built a wooden floor in this second cabin with a secret trap door. The trap door led to a crevice in a granite ledge beneath the floor and then a dense thicket of prickly ash. It could thus serve as an escape route. Ann hacked a narrow trail through the thicket so she and her children could flee from their cabin unseen. The crevice in the granite ledge still exists today, as well as the prickly ash thicket.

The trees the Story family could handle were so small that they yielded poles rather than logs, but the poles were still adequate to build a satisfactory cabin. Once Ann chinked the cracks between the poles with mud and moss, the cabin was snug enough to hold heat in and keep the weather out.

Keeping the weather out was one thing; keeping raiding Indians out was another. Ann knew she could not defend the cabin against another Indian raid or an attack by British troops. Her only chance would be to hide the children again. But the flooded swamp could be reached by canoe only when the water happened to be very high. She needed a better hiding place. Then an idea occurred to her.

Assembling her children in the canoe, Ann paddled upstream a few hundred yards and nosed the canoe toward a high sloping bank on the western shore, the far side of the stream from her cabin. After disembarking, she started to dig into the bank. Along with her children, Ann dug a horizontal tunnel at the waterline. River water flooded the tunnel floor. The opening to the tunnel was just large enough to slide the canoe inside, with the family lying down in the canoe. Past the opening, they widened the tunnel into an underground cave that was long enough to hold the canoe.

The Storys dumped the dirt from their cave into Otter Creek, so they would leave no telltale signs of digging. Then they hid the entrance to the cave by sticking bushes in front of it. They would remove the bushes only when passing in or out. Since they would travel to and from the cave by canoe, they would leave no tracks to show their hiding place. The cavern was in an inconspicuous location, because travelers moving overland usually journeyed on the other side of the creek. Moreover, the cave was on an outside bend of the creek, and canoeists usually paddled near inside bends to shorten their trip.

Inside the tunnel, the Story family dug a shelf above the water and to one side, creating a platform wide enough for them all to sleep upon, with extra space to store food and other valuables. Tangled roots from the trees above helped hold the dirt ceiling in place. In this underground room, Ann's family slept safely every night. In the morning they returned to their homestead across the creek, worked in the fields, and prepared their meals in the cabin. They spent their nights in the cave, hidden from their enemies.

Her secret cavern made Ann even more valuable to the Green Mountain Boys, who could store gunpowder and supplies there with little risk of discovery. Impressed by her cleverness, Green Mountain Boy leaders grew to trust Ann, seeking advice and intelligence information from her whenever they traveled through her area. She became a friend of Ethan Allen, as well as his spy. Her children helped her gather information. They took turns watching Otter Creek and were always on the lookout for enemies traveling through the area.

Although they lived in a lonely cabin on the frontier, important events in the colonial cities affected Ann's family. In Philadelphia, delegates at the Second Continental Congress wanted to form alliances with European governments that supported their rebellion against England. But Congress could not form any alliances until it had created a separate government. The boldest patriot spokesmen convinced their colleagues to formally declare independence.

A fiery rebel named Thomas Jefferson was selected to write the Declaration of Independence. A defiant pamphlet that Jefferson had previously published, "Summary of the Rights of British America," had revealed his writing abilities as well as his political ideas. For days Jefferson worked on the independence document, choosing his words carefully and writing many revisions. He submitted the document on June 28, and after much editing by his associates, the Declaration of Independence was signed by the patriot leaders on July 4, 1776.

The famous second paragraph of the Declaration of Independence is believed to be mostly Jefferson's wording:

> "We hold these truths to be self-evident: that all men are created equal; that they are endowed by their creator with certain inalienable rights; that among these are life, liberty, and the pursuit of happiness; that to secure these rights, governments are instituted among men, deriving their just powers from the consent of the governed; that whenever any form of government becomes destructive of those ends, it is the right of the people to alter or to abolish it, and to institute new government, laying its foundations on such principles, and organizing its powers in such form, as to them shall seem most likely to effect their safety and happiness."

We can only imagine what Ann Story thought of the phrase "all men are created equal," with no mention of women. But the word sexism had not even been invented at that time, and the Declaration of Independence was so radical that it shocked the British authorities and excited the imagination of American patriots. Encouraged by the Declaration, the rebels rallied around the idea of independence. With the Declaration of Independence, Ann Story became even more determined to fight for liberty.

CHANCE ENCOUNTERS

Many historians believe that a baby crying in the night brought about Ann Story's most important contribution to the fight for independence. According to their accounts, one of Ann's younger sons came running to her one morning. He had found a woman in the woods, he told her excitedly, sitting in the wilderness alone and crying.

Curious, Ann wondered where the woman had come from. What she was doing so far from any town? Could she be acting as bait in a trap set by Tories? On guard against a trick, Ann decided to investigate.

Ann's son led her to a place where they could see the woman without being seen themselves. Ann observed the woman for a long time, watchful for any sign of enemies, but she spotted no one hiding in ambush. The woman had a big belly that shook with her sobs, and Ann soon realized that the woman was pregnant.

Feeling sorry for her, Ann cautiously walked toward the woman and greeted her. The woman's jaw dropped in shock, then she stood up to hug Ann, tearfully thanking God that she had been saved.

When the woman calmed down enough to speak clearly, she told Ann that she had been captured by a band of Indians. Under orders from the British in Canada, the Indians had raided the settlement of Pittsford and taken several captives. The Indians drove their victims north toward Canada, where the British would pay them a ransom for colonial prisoners. Eager to avoid an encounter with the Green Mountain Boys, the Indians urged the captives on at top speed. The pregnant woman had had trouble keeping up with the fast pace.

Although she was afraid of the Indians, the woman told Ann that she was even more afraid of being deserted in the middle of the wild woods, where she would probably starve to death. She had tried hard to keep up, but she had slipped farther and farther behind. Finally the Indians had trotted out of sight, not bothering to drop back and kill her.

Left in the wilderness, the poor woman sank to the ground and wept for herself and her unborn child. Her imagination got the better of her, and she had been overcome by fear of being eaten by a panther or wolves. She had given up hope by the time Ann found her.

Ann took the woman to her homestead and welcomed her into the Story home. When it came time for the baby to be born, Ann calmed the expectant mother's fears, pointing out that she herself had five healthy children. Ably serving as a mid-wife, Ann helped the woman deliver a fine son. The baby was born in the pole cabin, but soon Ann moved him and his mother to the secret cavern for safety.

Around this time Tories had been snooping around the Grants settlements, gathering as much information as they could about the Green Mountain Boys to help the British. When they had collected valuable information about the locations and defenses of the Grants villages, a group of them headed toward Canada. To avoid discovery by the Green Mountain Boys, the Tories split up as they left the Grants settlements, planning to regroup on the frontier before the final leg of their journey.

One of the Tory spies was a man named Ezekiel Jenny. Traveling under cover of darkness, Jenny followed Otter Creek downstream, moving toward his meeting with the other Tories. Suddenly he heard a strange sound in the pitch-black forest. Stopping to listen, he heard the noise again. It sounded like a baby crying. The faint noise seemed to be coming from underground on the far side of the stream.

Ezekiel Jenny was puzzled. Then he remembered that Ann Story's cabin was nearby, and he suspected that he had found the Story family's nighttime hiding place. Knowing Ann was a trusted agent of the Green Mountain Boys, Jenny thought that if he questioned her, he might be able to get more information for the British. He decided that the chance was too good to pass up, so he delayed his journey for a few hours and hid in the bushes beside Otter Creek, waiting for dawn.

As the sky grew lighter, Jenny saw something move on the far shore. Bushes slid aside and a canoe emerged onto Otter Creek. Recognizing the Story family in the canoe, Jenny smiled. He followed them downstream to their homestead, waited until they landed, then stepped into view.

Ann knew who Ezekiel Jenny was, and when he asked her questions about the Green Mountain Boys, she was careful to avoid telling him anything important. Her lack of cooperation made Jenny angry. Red in the face, he threatened to shoot her if she did not give him some straight answers. He cocked his rifle and pointed it at Ann's chest.

Ann glared at Jenny and calmly told him that she was not afraid of being shot by a complete coward like him. He threatened and yelled, but Ann stood firm. Finally, Jenny gave up and slunk away downstream.

Ann watched him leave, certain that he was up to no good, and decided to warn the Green Mountain Boys about the incident. She wanted to send Solomon to them with a message, so she searched her cabin for something to write on. Paper was scarce on the frontier, and the only paper in her cabin was the pages in her family Bible. Believing that the Lord would understand, Ann tore the flyleaf from her Bible and wrote her message on it.

Thrilled to be trusted with such a grave responsibility, Solomon ran to Middlebury. He delivered the note to a Green Mountain Boy named Daniel Foot, who spread the word to Samuel Bentley, Captain James Bentley, and other nearby Whigs. They formed a posse of about a dozen Green Mountain Boys. Solomon volunteered to join and was excited and a little scared when they agreed to let him go along.

The Green Mountain Boys hurried north after Ezekiel Jenny, and when they thought that they were about to overtake him, they slowed down. Staying out of sight, they followed Jenny to Monkton, where he met up with the rest of his band of Tories, including their leader, Benjamin Cole. Confident that they were unobserved, the fourteen Tory spies made a comfortable camp with a cozy fire.

When the Tories were sound asleep around their campfire, the Green Mountain Boys rushed in, completely surprising them, and captured the entire band without any casualties. The posse marched their captives to Neshobe (where the town of Brandon now stands). There a Whig "court" made up of Green Mountain Boys Thomas Tuttle, John Smith, Timothy Barker, Moses Oldstead, and Jonathan Rowley questioned them for two and a half days. The Tories eventually admitted their plot. Then the Green Mountain Boys marched them to Fort Ticonderoga, where they were imprisoned.

The adventure was the beginning of Solomon Story's successful career as a Green Mountain Boy, but the most important result of this episode was that the British did not receive the vital information from the Tory spies. If they had received it, they might have been able to conquer the Grants region. The history of the American Revolution would have been very different.

And Ann Story, who already had a deserved reputation as a brave mother and honest patriot, became famous as a clever agent for the Green Mountain Boys whose calmness under pressure defeated a Tory plot and helped capture fourteen enemy spies.

NEW BEGINNINGS

Each year at their homestead in Salisbury, Ann and her family expanded their fields to produce more crops. But during the dead of winter, Otter Creek froze over, making their secret cavern useless because they could not reach it by canoe. Tracks in the snow on top of the iced-over stream would have revealed their hideout. So Ann moved her family for a few months each winter to the northern edge of Rutland, near the Pittsford town line. They stayed at Simeon Chafy's farm during the coldest part of winter, then returned to their cabin as soon as the ice melted on Otter Creek.

Ann always welcomed the Green Mountain Boys who passed her way. As the Revolutionary War continued, rebel soldiers and war refugees who traveled along Otter Creek knew that they could find a safe place to rest and a good meal at the Story cabin.

For a while the war went poorly for the rebels. Thirty thousand British troops assembled in August 1776 and attacked New York, intending to take control of the Hudson River, which was the best route between Canada and the patriot strongholds. The British plan was to divide the rebel forces and defeat northern New York first, then attack the southern region.

The Continental army lacked the firepower to beat the British in a decisive battle, so General George Washington harassed them with minor attacks for months, never risking a major assault. By staying just beyond the reach of a telling blow, Washington bought a little time for his ragged rebel army, but finally he grew desperate. In the spring of 1777, the British seemed ready to win.

The patriots needed a victory to boost their spirits, so Washington scraped together six thousand men and attacked at dawn the day after Christmas. He surprised the enemy troops at Trenton, capturing one thousand soldiers and many much-needed supplies. Soon the Continental Army won a bloody victory at Princeton, which encouraged more people to join the revolution. Recruits poured in during the spring and summer, and by September 1777 Washington had sixteen thousand men.

Then the rebel fortunes took another bad turn. The British captured Philadelphia, inflicting heavy losses on the Continental Army. Washington retreated to Valley Forge to lick his wounds.

Meanwhile, the land dispute in the Grants continued. Finally, the Grants settlers grew so frustrated by the conflicting claims of New York, New Hampshire, and others that they decided to declare themselves an independent republic. In January 1777 seventy-two delegates from Grants towns unanimously voted to name their new domain "The Republic of Vermont." Ann Story cheered this decision, believing that the Grants settlers deserved to control their own destiny. Ever since she was a young girl, she had believed in the virtues and rewards of hard work. She had worked hard to build a home for her family, and she did not want her fate to be controlled by faraway strangers. Local government made more sense to her. Ann proudly declared herself a Vermonter.

Immediately the new republic faced danger. A new British army of almost ten thousand men was moving south on Lake Champlain, intending to join forces with the larger British army. British artillery troops were able to drag their cannon to the top of a steep hill overlooking Fort Ticonderoga, gaining a commanding position over the Americans in the fort. The patriots were forced to desert the fort, and they retreated south.

The American retreat left most of western Vermont north of Manchester unprotected. A few militia soldiers stayed at forts in Castleton, Rutland, and Pittsford, but most of the settlers fled south, away from the threat of the British army. Vermont was thrown into confusion.

Refugees left homeless by the war wandered aimlessly, seeking shelter. Soldiers who had fought bravely for America went unpaid, and food was scarce. Grieving widows and other relatives of soldiers who had died for their country caught diseases spread by refugee and troop movements. Vermont officials struggled to keep their young republic alive.

Through it all, Ann kept her family together and safe. Somehow they avoided catching any fatal diseases, and the British army passed by on their west. The British caught up with the rear guard of retreating Americans at Hubbardton. There the Green Mountain Boys and other patriots fought bravely, delaying the British advance long enough to avoid a rout, but more than two hundred

Americans were killed, and hundreds more were captured.

To slow the British march toward Albany, the retreating Americans dropped hundreds of trees across the trail. The British had to clear the road to move their artillery and supplies, slowing their progress to a mile a day. When British food supplies grew low, they decided to raid the Bennington militia stockpile. A force of about fifteen hundred redcoats marched to capture the Yankee supplies.

Even though they had neither cannon nor bayonets, the Americans won a great victory at Bennington, taking down almost a thousand British troops while losing only about fifty men themselves. They captured several cannon and many rifles and other supplies and severely damaged the British effort.

Recognizing an opportunity to crush the northern British army, General Washington sent as many troops as he could spare to join the American forces at Albany. The patriot army won a major victory at Saratoga, accepting the British surrender on October 17, 1777.

Then in a daring raid the Green Mountain Boys recaptured Fort Ticonderoga. It was a great relief to Ann Story, since it meant that her frontier homestead was no longer behind enemy lines. She and her family were able to settle down to a routine of productive homesteading for a few years. As her sons grew older, they joined the Green Mountain Boys to help defend the area, but they still lived at home and helped work the farm.

George Washington's men survived the miserable winter of 1777–1778 at Valley Forge. They lacked everything, even the most basic supplies, and many of them had to stand on their tattered hats in the snow when they were on sentry duty, because they had no boots. But they held on, encouraged by the news that the King of France had agreed to an alliance with the United States of America.

Many American citizens did not want assistance from France or any other foreign power, but the French had something that the Americans needed: a powerful navy. Moreover, the French alliance weakened support for the British in Canada, where many citizens felt a bond with France. In June 1779 Spain also declared war on England, which diminished popular support for the war in England, once the British soldiers were fighting French and Spaniards as well as Americans.

Despite these hopeful signs, the outcome of the American Revolution was still very much in doubt. Many desertions and a lack of supplies eroded the Continental Army's morale and strength. Then a fresh French fleet arrived with reinforcements in 1781.

The French fleet occupied Chesapeake Bay, trapping the British in Yorktown, denying them reinforcements or supplies by ship. A combined force of Americans and French attacked Yorktown, and the British eventually surrendered to Washington in October 1781. The Treaty of Paris, signed on September 3, 1783, officially recognized the independence of the United States of America. George Washington tried to retire but was called upon to serve as the first president of the United States.

By the end of the war, Solomon Story and his brothers Ephraim and Samuel were respected Green Mountain Boys who could be counted on to defend their community. Many settlers moved into Vermont, attracted by the available land and the strong economy, which was not saddled with war debts like the struggling United States. Susanna and Hannah were growing into young women. In her early forties, Ann was an attractive woman firmed by years of farm work. The Story homestead became more productive as the family members reaped the rewards of their labors.

One by one Ann's children left home to begin lives of their own. She was sad to see them go, but she was proud of her children and wanted them to enjoy life to the fullest. By the year 1788, Solomon and Ephraim were both property owners in Salisbury, fulfilling Amos and Ann's dream.

New York still quarreled with Vermont over the disputed land and New York ships refused to carry Vermont goods to the European markets. Some Vermonters formed business ties with Quebec. They successfully traded timber and livestock for manufactured goods from England, shipped through Quebec.

Vermont eventually settled the land dispute by paying $30,000 to the people who held the old New York land patents. In January 1791, by a margin of 105 to 2, Vermont delegates voted to join the United States. Congress voted to accept Vermont as the fourteenth state on March 4, 1791.

Shortly after Vermont became a state, Benjamin Smalley, the man who had helped Solomon bury Amos, became a widower. After mourning for his deceased wife Martha, Benjamin proposed to Ann Story. Ann's daughters were both married by this time, so there were no family responsibilities holding her back. In 1792, at the age of fifty-one, Ann became Mrs. Benjamin Smalley.

ELDERLY ANN

Ann and Benjamin Smalley moved to a farm in Middlebury, near Benjamin's original homestead (where Amos Story was buried). Some historians spell Benjamin's last name "Smauley," but the old gravestones and memorials spell it "Smalley." Benjamin was a leading citizen who took an active role in town affairs. In 1773 he had made his pitch on two hundred acres at the mouth of the Middlebury River, where it empties into Otter Creek. He was perhaps as bold as Ann—Benjamin Smalley and Daniel Foot were the only settlers of Middlebury and Cornwall who did not retreat south in June 1776. That year, Benjamin lost all of his movable property to Indian raids. He left in September, but he stubbornly returned the following winter with his family. They replaced the original cabin with a nice frame house in 1783.

Benjamin was sixty-seven years old when he married Ann, sixteen years her senior. Thirteen years after they married, Benjamin's health took a turn for the worse.

Weakened by old age, Benjamin decided to return to his original homestead, where his son Imri was living. He and Ann moved in with Imri in 1805. Benjamin passed away in 1807 at the age of eighty-two.

A white marble monument, weathered and flecked with green moss, still stands on the site of Benjamin's homestead in Middlebury. The tall rounded stone gracefully tapers to a point, atop a round gristmill stone. The inscription reads: "Near this place B. Smalley built the first house in town, 1773. He married Widow Story."

Benjamin Smalley had owned plenty of real estate, more than almost anyone in the area, but he was also deeply in debt. After he died, Ann discovered that Benjamin owed more money than she could raise by selling the land. At the age of sixty-six, Ann was suddenly bankrupt.

Still stubbornly independent, she politely declined offers of assistance from her family and friends, refusing to accept charity from her loved ones. Nor did she want to rely on welfare from the government. She had little left except her dignity and her pride, which she intended to keep. Never a stranger to hard work, she managed to support herself for the next four years by serving as a midwife and a caretaker for old and sick people.

While Ann was struggling to get by, trouble developed again between England and the United States. English ships seized American ships on the high seas, upsetting the transportation of American goods. The United States reacted by stopping all trade with England and Canada. This was hard on the Green Mountain State, because most Vermont products were marketed through Quebec. Many Vermonters reacted by breaking the law, smuggling their goods across the northern border.

When the United States declared war on England in 1812, most Vermont citizens opposed the war because they needed to trade with Canada and England. Shutting down the Quebec trade had been hard on Vermont, and during the war the economic situation worsened. The University of Vermont was closed in 1813 when the buildings were needed to shelter soldiers and supplies. Battles were fought on both sides of Lake Champlain, and on the water too. The fighting reached a climax in September 1814, when American forces soundly defeated the British fleet on Lake Champlain. The War of 1812 officially ended when the Treaty of Ghent was signed in December 1814.

The declaration of war in 1812 was not the most important event of the year for Ann, however. At the age of seventy-one, she was married for the third time, to Captain Stephen Goodrich.

Stephen had made his pitch in 1784 on two hundred acres east of Middlebury Village with his two sons. In 1800 Stephen traded some of that land for a farm on the southern border of Middlebury. He was an eighty-two-year-old widower when he asked for Ann's hand.

After the wedding, Ann moved to Captain Goodrich's successful farm, where she enjoyed her last years. She died at their home in Middlebury on April 5, 1817. The exact cause of her death is unknown, but she reportedly died peacefully of "old age."

Ann was laid to rest in the Farmingdale Cemetery in Middlebury, sometimes called the Seeley District Cemetery or the District No. 1 graveyard. Her marble headstone was carved to read: "Mrs. Hannah Goodrich Wife of Capt. Stephen Goodrich Died 5th April 1817 in the 75th year of her age."

LEGACY

In later years, some historians worried that people might become confused about the location of Ann's grave, since her headstone read "Mrs. Hannah Goodrich." To solve that problem, the following words were added to her tombstone:

Formerly Ann Story
The Heroine of Thompson's Green Mountain Boys
Inscribed by the Ann Story Chapter DAR
of Rutland VT 1898

The word "Thompson's" refers to Judge D. P. Thompson, author of a popular book called *The Green Mountain Boys.*

A few years later, the Vermont Society of Colonial Dames set up a monument in honor of Ann Story. The monument stands in Salisbury on the site of her frontier home. The land was donated from the estate of Columbus Smith, and the stone was donated by Fletcher D. Proctor. The monument is carved from Sutherland Falls marble, and it weighs about ten thousand pounds. The monument reads:

ON THIS SPOT STOOD THE HOME
OF
ANN STORY
IN GRATEFUL MEMORY OF HER
SERVICE IN THE STRUGGLE OF
THE GREEN MOUNTAIN BOYS FOR
THE INDEPENDENCE OF VERMONT
ERECTED BY
THE VERMONT SOCIETY OF
COLONIAL DAMES
MAY 30, 1905
DEDICATED JULY 27 1905

The Mary Baker Allen chapter of the Daughters of the American Revolution dedicated another monument to Ann's memory on August 26, 1914. This Vermont marble monument was placed in Cornwall on the site of Ann's secret cave. The monument reads: "This marks the site of Ann Story's cave used as a place of refuge against the invasion of Tories and Indians. Erected in honor of and for her loyalty to the Green Mountain Boys by Mary Baker Allen Chapter, Daughters of the American Revolution, Cornwall, Vermont." Workers who set up the stone reported uncovering an underground hollow measuring three feet by nine feet, which they believed was the remains of Ann's hideout. Katharine Griswold, a DAR historian, wrote a long poem honoring Ann Story, which she read at the dedication ceremony. This poem and other memorials to Ann Story may be seen at the Vermont Historical Society in Montpelier.

The legend of Ann Story continued to impress later generations of Vermonters. A tale of Ann's adventures was broadcast on the radio as part of the *This is Vermont* series, which aired from 1948 through 1950. The radio program was called "Ann Story, Mother of a State."

Two centuries after Ann Story faced danger on the frontier, the Salisbury–Leicester Historical Society honored her memory with a Bicentennial project. A log cabin that another pioneer had built in Addison in 1772 was taken apart and hauled to Salisbury, then rebuilt where Ann Story's cabins had stood. The Historical Society held a dedication ceremony on July 17, 1976. A composer named Gene Childers wrote "The Ballad of Ann Story," which was performed at the ceremony. Seeley Reynolds read the dedication address.

Seeley Reynolds, who served as Vermont state senator from Addison County from 1974 through 1982, is a descendant of Ann Story on both sides of his family tree. His grandmother, Grace Seeley, was a direct descendant of Ann Story on the Story side. Grace married George Reynolds, and years later, when they were researching their genealogy, they discovered that he was descended from the Reynolds side of Ann's family!

The various headstone materials at the Farmingdale Cemetery, where Ann Story is buried, show the progression of time. The oldest graves on the western edge are unmarked, because their wooden markers have long since rotted away. The next oldest graves in the middle are identified by marble headstones, worn and mossy. Ann lies in this section, between Captain Stephen Goodrich and Rachel Smalley, wife of Benjamin's son Alfred. The newer graves on the east have shiny headstones of Vermont granite.

Seeley Reynolds, his wife Anna, and their thirty descendants were worried that the words on Ann Story's headstone might fade away, so they purchased another stone. Cut to the same size as the original stone, this piece of Virginia slate is mounted flush with the marble, supported by a base buried four feet deep. The words are the same as the original except for the bottom two lines, which say: "Preserved by the S. Seeley Reynolds JR family in 1991."

Seeley and Anna's grandchildren live within a mile and a half of Ann Story's cabin, two hundred years and nine generations after Ann pioneered the area.

Many brave women faced danger and hardships on the American frontier. Most of their names have been forgotten over the years. Ann Story's tale endures because she lived in a time and place where important events happened, and because she had the courage and resourcefulness to make a memorable difference.

Chronology

Date	Ann Story	Vermont	North America
1741	Hannah (Ann) Reynolds was born in Connecticut.		
1749		Wentworth started the New Hampshire Grants.	
1755	Ann married Amos Story.		
1759			Wolfe conquered Quebec, Sept. 13.
1765		Grants settlers defied New York surveyors.	
1774	Amos and Solomon go to Salisbury.		
1775	Amos Story died.	Ethan Allen captured Fort Ticonderoga, May.	The battles of Concord and Lexington were fought, April.
1776	Indians burned the Story cabin.		The Declaration of Independence was signed, July 4.
1777		Vermont declared itself an independent republic, Jan. 17.	
1791		Vermont became the fourteenth state.	
1792	Ann married Benjamin Smalley.		
1799			George Washington died.

|------|-----------|---------|---------------|
1808	Ann became a widow again.		
1812	Ann married Captain Stephen Goodrich.		The United States declared war on England.
1814		The British were defeated on Lake Champlain.	
1817	Ann died on April 5.		

Bibliography

Caulkins, Frances Manwaring. *History of Norwich, Connecticut.* Hartford, 1874.

Cheney, Cora. *Vermont, the State with the Storybook Past.* The New England Press, 1986.

Duffy, John. *Vermont: An Illustrated History.* Windsor Publications, 1985.

Hahn, Michael T. *Ethan Allen: A Life of Adventure.* The New England Press, 1994.

Hibbert, Christopher. *Redcoats And Rebels.* Avon Books, 1991.

Jackson, Edgar N. *Green Mountain Hero.* Lantern Press, 1961.

Johnson, Neil. *The Battle of Lexington and Concord.* Four Winds Press, 1992.

Nordstrom, Judy. *Concord and Lexington.* Dillon Press, 1993.

Petersen, James E. *Otter Creek: The Indian Road.* Dunmore House, 1990.

Sunderland, Edwin S. *The Home of the Mother of a State.* Stowell, 1914.

Swift, Samuel. *History of the Town of Middlebury.* Charles E. Tuttle, 1971.

Thompson, Judge Daniel P. *Green Mountain Boys.* John W. Lovell, 1839.

Weeks, John M. *History of Salisbury.* A. H. Copeland, 1860.